Introduction

Welcome to the latest installment of TOKYOPOP Sneaks, your insider's guide to the wild and wonderful world of manga!

As you may already know, manga – the Japanese word for comics– has become a truly global phenomenon. All over the world, readers can't get enough of its irresistible visual storytelling and bleeding-edge graphic design. There's manga for every taste, too: science fiction, romance, comedy, fantasy, action...you name it and TOKYOPOP has it covered!

Within the pages of this book, you will find an extraordinary selection of TOKYOPOP's latest titles that are sure to fire your imagination like nothing you have ever read before. Once you pick out your favorites, remember that TOKYOPOP manga is available everywhere books are sold.

From all of us here at TOKYOPOP, thank you for your support – and welcome to the Manga Revolution!

left to right ⟶ left to right ⟶ left to right

TABLE OF CONTENTS

The Story:

Raise an army. Rule the world. Only one can be Archlord! In this classic tale of a hero who must fulfill his destiny, a father takes his newborn son on a journey to be named. But when fortune and loyalty give way to betrayal and greed, it's up to an unlikely champion and one remarkable sword to restore honor and balance to the land! Based on the hit video game.

The Creator:

Jin-Hwan Park

ACTION FANTASY

T
TEEN
AGE 13+

£6.99

Episode4
Ugdrasil

HIYAH!

GEHK!

HEY, MR. CHEAPSHOT! HOW ABOUT TWO OUT OF THREE?!

CHEATER...

HOW DO YOU LEARN THAT STUFF, ANYWAY?

YOU MAY HAVE HUMAN BLOOD IN YOU...

A HALF ORC?!

...BUT THE ORC IN YOU IS...ORCISH. A LOT OF ORC. TOO MUCH, MAYBE.

The fate of the Mana Tree Lies in your hands!

NINTENDO**DS**.Lite

SQUARE ENIX

From the creators of FINAL FANTASY comes a new, epic adventure! Cross blades with evil to save the holy Mana Tree. Go it alone or team up with three companions in wireless multiplayer mode. Brace yourself and enter the world of CHILDREN of MANA.

TOKYOPOP®
· PRESENTS ·

the dreaming

The Story:

Twin sisters Amber and Jeanie enroll in an Australian boarding school. But shortly after school begins, the twins uncover a dark, mysterious secret: Students have been known to walk off into the surrounding bushlands, where they vanish completely, without a trace!

The Creator:

Queenie Chan

DRAMA
HORROR

T
TEEN
AGE 13+

SRP:

£6.99

Chapter 3
The Dreaming

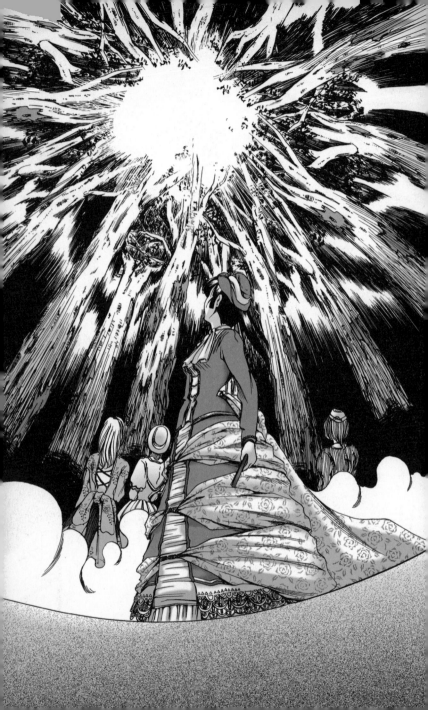

MAKING YOUR PASSION PORTABLE

WORLD OF WARCRAFT
TRADING CARD GAME

THROUGH THE
DARK PORTAL

◇ Contains brand-new The Burning Crusade™ content including armor, weapons, and the two new races, Blood Elves and Draenei.

◇ Three new Loot™ card items now available! Look for a new blanket, pet or fortune-telling imp for your online World of Warcraft® character.

◇ Supported by extensive Organized Play events such as Release Celebrations, Sneak Previews and exciting Darkmoon Faire tournaments worldwide.

Go to your local hobby store or visit
WWW.UDE.COM/WOW

NO. I'D RATHER KILL RATS.

With millions of players online, World of Warcraft has made gaming
history — and now's it's never been easier to join the adventure.
Simply visit **www.warcraft.com**, download the FREE TRIAL and join
thousands of mighty heroes for ten days of bold online adventure.

MASSIVELY EPIC ONLINE

The Story:

Tian and Drei von Richenstein, two unlikely heroes, embark on an adventure filled with excitement, intrigue, and absolute hilarity! Their journies are complicated by the fact that they have a knack for making allies into new enemies, mainly because their heroism and sense of adventure is topped only by their insatiable lust for gold. The funniest fantasy farce ever to grace a graphic novel!

The Creator:

Story by: Creative Hon
Art by: Yong-Wan Kwon

COMEDY FANTASY

TEEN
AGE 13+

SRP:

£6.99

OH, AN! 'RE ILL RE !

UH, YEAH. WE WERE JUST ABOUT TO LEAVE... WHY? WHAT'S UP, BBOBBEE?

OH, NOTHING. I WAS JUST BRINGING MY FATHER HIS MEDICATION.

YOU MUST VE JUST BEEN TO SEE HIM.

?

WELL, I GUESS KEEPING IT A SECRET FROM YOU IS SILLY, REALLY.

HEY, TIAN! I GOT THE TALONS, TOO!

BBOBBEE?

HELLO.

WHAT'S IN THE BAG?

THIS BAG?

?

TIAN? WHAT'S WRONG? ARE YOU HUNGRY OR SOMETHING?

UH-OH.

YOUR TINY BALLS DON'T IMPRESS ME! LET'S SEE JUST HOW HOT I CAN MAKE YOU!

......

HERE IT COMES!!!

NO ESCAPE!
WHEREVER YOU ARE.

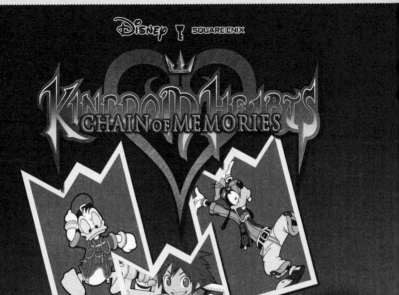

The Story:

Finney Bleak lives in a world of horror—literally. His family are ghosts, his classmates are monsters, and Finney is the most normal kid in school. But within the halls of Mephisto Prep, normal is the new weird and Finney dangles from the lowest rung of the social evolutionary ladder.

Then along comes Jenny. Smart. Beautiful. And totally into Finney. Only problem is, she's kind of dead. Jenny may be the ethereal object of Finney's affection, but their corporeal differences keep them apart. As if young romance wasn't awkward enough, try getting frisky with a ghost.

Just how far will Finney go to be with his true love? Let's just say not even Death can stand in his way!

The Creator:

Eric Wight

COMEDY FANTASY

T
TEEN
AGE 13+

SRP:

£6.99

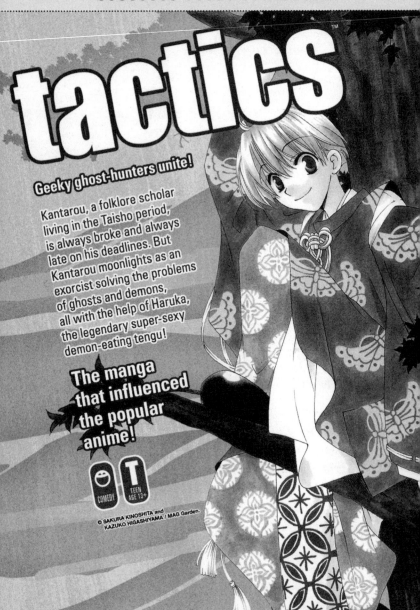

"YOU CAN'T AVOID FALLING UNDER ITS CHARM."
-IGN.COM

Sometimes even two's a crowd.

The manga phenomenon returns! It's year two for Christie at the Con, and the drama heats up. Matt is back, too—but who is that with him? Christie's mind may be on manga, but her heart is still with Matt. Between new significant others, new artists and the same old crazy fans, will these two star-crossed lovers ever find true romance?

CREATED BY SVETLANA CHMAKOVA!

FOR MORE INFORMATION VISIT: WWW.TOKYOPOP.CO.UK

RECAST ™

The Story:

JD lives a peaceful life with his grandfather on a small island, until bounty hunters show up looking for them! Will JD be able to put to use what his grandfather's taught him to survive in a world of magical peril? And what is the nature of the Recast spell his grandfather's cast on him?

The Creator:

Seung-Hui Kye

 ACTION FANTASY

 T TEEN AGE 13+

SRP:

£6.99

GRANDPA!

Cough!

Trying his best to look pitiful.

WHAT'S GOING ON, GRANDPA?!

DON'T COME NEAR ME!

?!

WHAT? THIS IS IT?

I REALLY HAD MY HOPES UP!

WHAT THE HECK IS GOING ON HERE?

WHO'S THE WEIRDO?

DID HE ATTACK GRANDPA?

ALL THE POWER IN THE WORLD, AND YOU CHOOSE A KNUCKLE BLADE?

I GUESS THAT WOULD APPEAL TO A HILLBILLY BOY LIKE YOU.

IS IT OKAY TO LEAVE HIM ALONE LIKE THAT?

JD NEEDS TO BE ABLE TO TAKE CARE OF HIMSELF.

OR ELSE THERE'S NO POINT IN ME USING THE RECAST ON HIM.

I SHOULD GO AFTER--

YOU DON'T NEED TO DO THAT!

WHY DON'T YOU JUST HELP ME GET THIS SPELL OFF?

LET ME HELP YOU UP...

HOLD IT!

WHERE DO YOU THINK YOU'RE GOING? I'M GOING TO FIGHT YOU.

TAKE THIS! PRETTY CUTIE PUNCH!

??

77

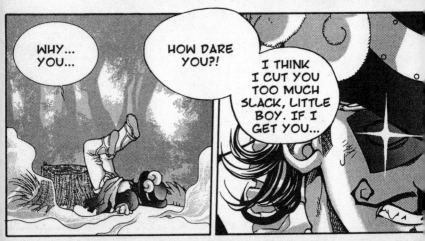

WHY... YOU...

HOW DARE YOU?!

I THINK I CUT YOU TOO MUCH SLACK, LITTLE BOY. IF I GET YOU...

The Story:

The Goblin King has kept a watchful eye on Toby: His minions secretly guiding and protecting the child... Legions of goblins work behind the scenes to ensure that Toby has whatever his heart desires... Preparing him for the day when he will return to the Labyrinth and take his rightful place beside Jareth as the heir to the Goblin Kingdom...

That day has come...

...but no one has told Toby.

The Creator:

Story by: Jake T. Forbes
Art by: Chris Lie

FANTASY

T
TEEN
AGE 13+

SRP:

£6.99

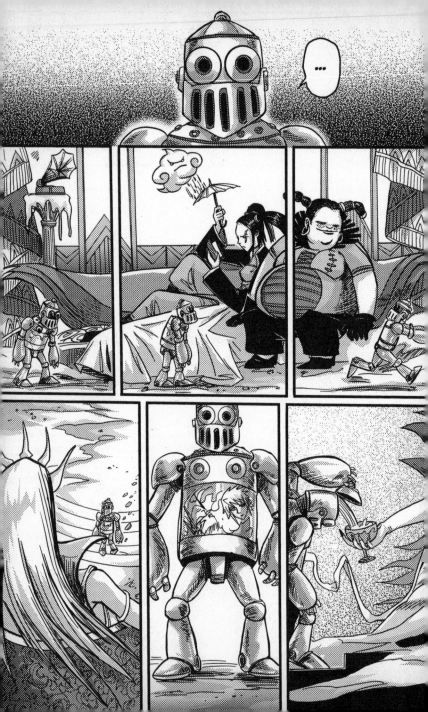

OH, GREAT. MOM'S HOME...

THE SCHOOL CALLED.

IT'S NOT TRUE! I SWEAR I DIDN'T CHEAT.

WHATEVER IT'S YOUR LIFE, TOBY.

HUH?

MACROWORD ™

The War of 1812
The Water was Important

I'VE GOT TO GET THIS HISTORY PAPER WRITTEN. I'VE BEEN PUTTING IT OFF FOR WEEKS.

I DON'T KNOW ABOUT THIS FONT... TIMES IS SO GENERIC.

GAH! WHAT AM I DOING?

NO NEED TO PANIC. I DID PRINT IT OUT BEFORE I LOST IT.

PRINT, DAMMIT! I KNOW I HIT "PRINT"!

YOU... YOU'RE WITH *HIM*, AREN'T YOU?!

GIVE THAT BACK!

STAR TREK

The Story:

Star Trek Goes Manga! Japanese-style sequential art combines with the most renowned science fiction franchise ever created to capture the spirit of the original series in a completely new way.

Ten artists and writers deliver tales of triumph aboard the original NCC-1701. Like the original TV series, these new journeys venture into the terrain of social politics, personal reflection...and bare-knuckled brawls between the dashing Captain Kirk and various indigenous beasts. Spock's unflappable logic, Bones' flare for drama, Scotty's perpetual struggle to keep the lights on...all come at you in a fresh, new style.

The Creator:

Story by: Joshua Ortega
Art by: Gregory Giovanni Johnson

SCI-FI

T
TEEN
AGE 13+

SRP:

£6.99

CAPTAIN'S LOG.
STARDATE 4010.6.
AFTER DELIVERING
MUCH-NEEDED MEDICAL
SUPPLIES TO MAKUS III,
THE ENTERPRISE HAS
SET A NEW COURSE--

SECTOR 061.
A LARGELY UNEXPLORED
REGION OF SPACE NEAR
THE ALEXISIAN SYSTEM.

IT'S
GOOD TO BE
BACK ON THE
FRONTIER.

CAPTAIN I'M RECEIVING A TRANSMISSION FROM THE NEAREST PLANET...

...BUT I DON'T UNDERSTAND THE MESSAGE...

IT'S STRANGE.

LET'S HEAR IT, UHURA.

I'VE NEVER HEARD ANYTHING LIKE IT.

CAPTAIN, IF I MAY?

OF COURSE, MR. SPOCK.

THIS SIGNAL-- I RECALL IT FROM MY STUDIES ON VULCAN.

IT IS A UNIQUE FREQUENCY THAT WAS ONCE USED BY THE HUMANOID INHABITANTS OF THE PLANET XIMEGA.

HOWEVER, THE XIMEGANS--AND THEIR CULTURE AND TECHNOLOGY--WERE PRESUMED TO HAVE BEEN DESTROYED WITH THEIR PLANET OVER ONE HUNDRED EARTH YEARS AGO.

I RECOMMEND FURTHER INVESTIGA-TION.

YOUR MIND NEVER CEASES TO AMAZE ME, SPOCK.

THIS IS TRUE, CAPTAIN-- THOUGH I THOUGHT YOU WOULD HAVE GROWN ACCUSTOMED TO IT BY NOW.

TAKING YOU FOR GRANTED WOULD BE THE LAST THING I'D WANT TO DO, MR. SPOCK.

MR. SULU, YOU HAVE THE BRIDGE.

SPOCK, BONES-- LET'S GET READY TO BEAM DOWN.

VSSH

WOOOOᵒᵒᵒ

WELCOME TO XIMEGA II.

HUH?

103

AND FINALLY, THIS IS OUR MANUAL LABOR PAVILION. A LIVING LINK TO OUR DISTANT PAST, WHERE WE ARE LEARNING--OR RATHER, RELEARNING--TO BE LESS RELIANT ON OUR ADVANCED TECHNOLOGY.

ZZRRR

CHARTEIL, IF YOU DON'T MIND MY ASKING--BY WHAT METHOD DID YOUR PEOPLE ARRIVE HERE?

I DIDN'T NOTICE ANY SPACECRAFT ON THE TOUR.

OH, WE... UNH...

CHARTEIL... ARE YOU OKAY?

YES, I... SUFFER FROM... HEADACHES SOMETIMES, BUT--

AAGH!!

ENDARCH!

OW-- BLAST IT!

GOOD GOD, MAN.

I'M FINE... IT'LL BE FINE.

FINE, MY EYE--THAT'S A SERIOUS WOUND YOU HAVE THERE!

YOU NEEDN'T CONCERN YOURSELF, DOCTOR.

I JUST... I JUST WANT TO GET BACK TO WORK.

MOTHER OF--

MY APOLOGIES AGAIN FOR ENDARCH'S BEHAVIOR. HE CAN BE A BIT... EMOTIONAL AT TIMES.

YOU DON'T HAVE TO APOLOGIZE.

THANK YOU.

SO--DID YOU MAKE UP YOUR MIND ABOUT OUR OFFER, CAPTAIN?

YES--WE ACCEPT.

AS LONG AS IT'S NO BURDEN TO YOU OR YOUR PEOPLE.

NOT AT ALL. JANEL HAS ALREADY PREPARED YOUR ACCOMODATIONS.

MR. SULU-- KIRK HERE. LOOKS LIKE WE'LL BE STAYING THE NIGHT.

LET'S KEEP AN OPEN CHANNEL, JUST TO BE SAFE.

BEEP BIP BEEP

WELL, THERE'S OBVIOUSLY SOMETHING PECULIAR GOING ON.

I AGREE, DR. McCOY.

YOU HEAR THAT, JIM? HE JUST AGREED WITH ME. YOU'RE MY WITNESS.

THAT WAS A JOKE, DOCTOR?

SARCASM, SPOCK. ALMOST A JOKE.

WHAT HAVE YOU NOTICED, BONES?

WELL, FOR ONE THING, THAT MAN WITH THE SAW, ENDER--

ENDARCH.

YES, THANK YOU, SPOCK.

HIS HAND HEALED WITHIN SECONDS.

I'VE NEVER SEEN PHYSIOLOGY LIKE THAT.

SPOCK? YOUR THOUGHTS?

AND SOMETHING ELSE--VERY STRANGE FOR A COLONY...

IT IS PUZZLING THAT CHARTEIL KNEW NOTHING ABOUT THE SIGNAL WE RECEIVED AND YET SEEMED TO ANTICIPATE OUR ARRIVAL.

THERE ARE NO CHILDREN. ANYWHERE. IF THEY'VE BEEN HERE FOR AS LONG AS CHARTEIL SAYS THEY HAVE...

NOT ANY COLONY THAT I'D LIKE TO BE A PART OF, I CAN TELL YOU THAT MUCH.

...WHY AREN'T THERE ANY CHILDREN? WHAT KIND OF A COLONY WOULDN'T REPRODUCE?

THE LOGICAL ANSWER IS THAT THIS IS A COLONY THAT *CANNOT* REPRODUCE.

IT'S WORTH GETTING TO THE BOTTOM OF. STAY ALERT TOMORROW.

INDEED, CAPTAIN.

MMM...THIS FOOD IS FANTASTIC.

I USUALLY DON'T ENJOY "OFF-WORLD" CUISINE, BUT YOU'RE RIGHT, JIM--THIS IS DAMN GOOD GRUB.

I ASSUMED CHARTEIL WOULD MEET US FOR BREAKFAST.

INDEED.

EXCUSE ME...? MAY I SPEAK WITH YOU FOR A MOMENT?

OF COURSE. PLEASE, HAVE A SEAT.

THANK YOU. MY NAME IS LIN.

NICE TO MEET YOU, LIN. I'M CAPTAIN JAMES T. KIRK.

A PLEASURE, GENTLEMEN.

AND THIS IS DR. MCCOY, THE SHIP'S PHYSICIAN, AND MR. SPOCK, OUR SCIENCE OFFICER.

YOU...YOU MUST HAVE RECEIVED THE SIGNAL.

YES-- MR. SPOCK RECOGNIZED IT AS XIMEGAN.

PREKRAFT WOULD HAVE ENJOYED SPEAKING WITH SOMEONE LIKE YOU, MR. SPOCK.

PREKRAFT?

YES. HE IS-- WAS--XIMEGA'S MOST BRILLIANT SCIENTIST. I WAS HIS ASSISTANT. I HELPED HIM WITH SOME OF THE MOLECULAR ASSEMBLY TECHNOLOGY... AND LAUNCHING THE ORIGINAL PROBE, THOUGH HE--

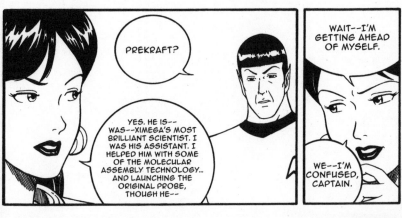

WAIT--I'M GETTING AHEAD OF MYSELF.

WE--I'M CONFUSED, CAPTAIN.

YOU SENT THE SIGNAL. THAT'S WHY CHARTEIL AND THE OTHERS WERE UNAWARE OF IT.

YES. I'VE SPOKEN TO OTHER XIMEGANS ABOUT MY FEELINGS, BUT THEY IGNORE ME, AND PREKRAFT WON'T SEE ANYONE, AND... I...I DIDN'T KNOW WHO TO TURN TO, SO I...

UNH...I... I HAVE TO GO NOW. I'M SORRY...

WE INTERRUPT THE MANGA TO BRING YOU THIS VERY IMPORTANT ANNOUNCEMENT:

pause

read right-to-left

If you've been enjoying the unforgettable left-to-right reading experience, we invite you to jump to the back of our manga mag for more cutting-edge manga...this time from Japan!

read left-to-right

If you've just soaked up the hottest manga from Japan, you need to turn to the front of our manga mag for some of TOKYOPOP's originally created manga and other cool articles.

Of course, if you're blown away by what you've been reading, then e-mail your friends, call your loved ones, and write the president—tell them all about the Manga Revolution!

And make sure you log on to www.TOKYOPOP.com for more manga!

HMM...IT'S HARD TO DESCRIBE.

WE LIKE TO JUMP AROUND A LOT, KEEP IT LOOSE.

WHAT KIND OF MUSIC?

PLASTIC CHEW...? NEVER HEARD OF IT.

NIRVANA HAS BEEN A MAJOR INFLUENCE.

WE'RE SIMPLE BUT EXPRESSIVE.

MAYBE YOU COULD CALL IT MELODIC OR DYNAMIC ROCK.

WE JUST PLAY WHATEVER WE LIKE. WE'RE A SMALL UNDERGROUND BAND, THAT'S ALL...

...EVEN BEFORE KURT.

LIKE GRUNGE? I THOUGHT THAT DIED IN THE EARLY '90's...

LIKE I SAID...WE DON'T JUST STICK TO ONE STYLE.

Introduction

Welcome to the latest installment of TOKYOPOP Sneaks, your insider's guide to the wild and wonderful world of manga!

As you may already know, manga – the Japanese word for comics– has become a truly global phenomenon. All over the world, readers can't get enough of its irresistible visual storytelling and bleeding-edge graphic design. There's manga for every taste, too: science fiction, romance, comedy, fantasy, action...you name it and TOKYOPOP has it covered!

Within the pages of this book, you will find an extraordinary selection of TOKYOPOP's latest titles that are sure to fire your imagination like nothing you have ever read before. Once you pick out your favorites, remember that TOKYOPOP manga is available everywhere books are sold.

From all of us here at TOKYOPOP, thank you for your support – and welcome to the Manga Revolution!

right to left ← right to left ← right to lef

TABLE OF CONTENTS

TOKYOPOP Sneaks UK 2007 vol. 1

Cover Art – Tomas Montalvo-Lagos
Graphic Design – Mike Estacio
Project Coordinators – Kasia Piekarz, Dennis McGuirk, Andrew Whelan and Rob Tokar
Digital Imaging Manager – Chris Buford
Pre-Press Manager – Erika Terriquez
Art Director – Anne Marie Horne
Managing Editor – Vy Nguyen
VP of Production – Ron Klamert
Editor-in-Chief – Rob Tokar
Publisher – Mike Kiley
President & C.O.O. – John Parker
C.E.O. & Chief Creative Officer – Stuart Levy

A  Manga

TOKYOPOP Inc.
5900 Wilshire Blvd. Suite 2000, Los Angeles, CA 90036
E-mail: info@TOKYOPOP.com
Come visit us online at www.TOKYOPOP.com
http://www.tokyopop.co.uk/

TOKYOPOP® SNEAKS

RIGHT-TO-LEFT CHEAT SHEET

This book is printed "manga-style," in the authentic Japanese right-to-left format. Since none of the artwork has been flipped or altered, readers get to experience the story just as the creator intended. You've been asking for it, so TOKYOPOP® delivered: authentic, hot-off-the-press, and far more fun!

DIRECTIONS

If this is your first time reading manga-style, here's a quick guide to help you understand how it works.

It's easy... just start in the top right panel and follow the numbers. Have fun, and look for more 100% authentic manga from TOKYOPOP®!

The Story:

In what had been a routine robbery, Cou, a young sky pirate, discovers Ren. A member of the Edel Raid race, Ren not only has the ability to lend Cou bizarre fighting capabilities, but is also the possessor of the Elemental Gelade stone that gives her powers beyond the norm. Together, they embark on a series of wild adventures that take them all over the world!

The Creator:

Mayumi Azuma

ACTION   FANTASY

T

TEEN
AGE 13+

SRP:
$6.99

DANG IT...
I HAVE
TO HURRY
AND SAVE
REN.

I HOPE
SHE'S ALL
RIGHT.

YEP...
I'M
LOST.

IS IT
SOMEHOW
DIFFERENT
IF SHE'S AN
EDEL RAID?

IT'S
TO SELL
THEM.

Yay!

WHY DOES
HE WANT
TO TAKE
GIRLS
ANYWAY?

DOES HE
JUST LIKE
WOMEN
THAT
MUCH?
DOES
HE MAKE
THEM
SERVE
HIM?

THAT OLD
GUY WAS
SAYING
HE WANTS
THEM MORE
IF THEY'RE
EDEL
RAIDS.

WHAT?

IT DETECTS ANY EDEL RAID WITHIN A ONE KM RADIUS.

CHECK IT OUT...I'VE ALREADY INPUTED REN'S DATA.

TADAH!!

ARC AILE

THE EDEL RAID RADAR THAT ARC AILE PROVIDES TO THE GOVERNMENT!

SO WHAT'S THIS FUZZY GUY?

THIS GREEN DOT HERE INDICATES REN'S LOCATION.

THIS RED DOT IS KUEA.

BUT HE WOULDN'T KEEP HIS MERCHANDISE JUST LYING AROUND....

REN WAS THE ONLY ONE THE TOWNSPEOPLE GAVE HIM.

THAT MEANS THAT INSIDE THIS BUILDING ...

FOLKS, THE ENEMY...

EH?

By the way, the □rst edition came with a carrying case.

IT'S AN UNIDENTIFIED EDEL RAID!

WHAT, THIS COLORLESS LIGHT ...?

WE HAVE KUEA!!

BUT NEVER FEAR !!

THAT'LL SHOW HIM!!

...IS AN EDEL RAID PLEASURE.

WHERE DID SHE GO?!

WHAT?! SHE'S GONE?!

BUT BOSS, IF HE CAN USE AN EDEL RAID...

Grrr...

...WE MIGHT END UP HAVING TO FIGHT ONE.

ENJOY ALL THIS DELISH FOOD? EASY... LIKE THIS! ♫

KUEA, AT A TIME LIKE THIS, HOW CAN YOU--

WE SHOULD LET KUEA FILL UP SO SHE'S READY TO FIGHT.

AW...I GUESS YOU'RE RIGHT.

WHOA...DID YOU S-SEE THAT?

YEAH.

?!!

THIS WAS YOUR DINNER, WAS IT?

OH... I GET IT. ♪

DUDE, IT'S *GOT* TO BE ILLEGAL TO KEEP PETS *THIS* BIG...!

ARE YOU SERIOUS ?!

I HOPE HE HAS A PERMIT.

NOW THAT I'M FULL AND IN A GOOD MOOD, I'LL BE EASY ON YOU. ♡

ISN'T THAT RIGHT, ROWEN? ♪

Y-YEAH. EASY.

THAT'S FINE. HERE KITTY, KITTY...! ♡

ポ O T

GAAH!!

WHEN KUEA EATS TOO MUCH, SHE GETS A LITTLE BELLIGERENT.

AAAGH!!

I CAN'T FIGHT THESE GUYS!

I CAME HERE TO SAVE REN!

COU!!

REN!!

C...
OU...

16

COU, WAIT!

WHAT DO YOU THINK REN IS?!

WEAPON ...?

OWNER ...?

DON'T RUSH IN UNTIL ROWEN GETS HERE!

LET GO OF ME!

YOU CAN'T! HE'S EQUIPPED WITH AN EDEL RAID!

IF YOU REALLY WANT HER BACK, COME AND GET HER.

WHAT ARE YOU MUTTERING ABOUT, BOY?

RUSHING IN NOW WOULD BE SUICIDE!

CONTROL YOURSELF!

WHAT'S WRONG, BOY?

AW...

SAY...

COME TO YOUR *DOOM.*

COME TO BEAZON...

...IS THAT YOUR WEAPON?

WARCRAFT
THE SUNWELL TRILOGY

GHOSTLANDS

THE CONCLUSION...
TO THE EPIC TRILOGY AWAITS...

The mighty Sunwell,
source of the high elves'
magical might, had been
thought lost...until now!
In the ruins of the
Ghostlands, a young
blue dragon and his
companions must fight
to save one of their own
from certain death.
But here, the dead
refuse to rest easy!

JAE-HWAN KIM,
ARTIST OF *KING OF HELL* AND
RICHARD A. KNAAK,
THE NEW YORK TIMES BEST-SELLING AUTHOR,
BRING YOU BACK TO
THE WORLD OF WARCRAFT!

ACTION

T
TEEN
AGE 13+

The Story:

It's a tale of magic and mistaken identity! Merleawe, who studies magic, is told her presence is needed for the sake of her country and persuaded by a handsome group of his loyal followers to pretend to be the Master Wizard Sylthfarn. Since she bears a strikingly identical resemblance to the Master Wizard, she fools everyone! Pretending to be Sylthfarn, she promises to protect the people. But will she be able to live up to those noble words?

The Creator:

Yuzu Mizutani

DRAMA FANTASY

TEEN
AGE 13+

SRP:
$6.99

BUT...

WHAT?

THE MASTER WIZARD SYLTHFARN, WHOSE NAME HAS SPREAD OVER EVERY CONTINENT, HAS RECENTLY GONE MISSING.

WHAT DOES THIS ALL MEAN?

!

WE CAN'T YET CONFIRM WHETHER HE IS ALIVE OR DEAD.

IF THIS INFORMATION WERE REVEALED TO THE PUBLIC...

...THERE WOULD BE MASS CONFUSION.

I can't behave like a boy!

...I AM A GIRL!

I'VE ONLY JUST BEGUN MY CLASSES— I KNOW LITTLE MAGIC.

AND EVEN IF I DO LOOK LIKE HIM...

EVEN I MISTOOK YOU FOR THE MASTER. YOU WON'T BE EASILY REVEALED.

IT'LL BE ALL RIGHT!

Fortunately you are no a very sex girl.

THAT MIGHT BE CONVENIENT FOR YOU!

UNTIL WE FIND HIM, WE WILL SUPPORT YOU IN EVERY POSSIBLE WAY SO LONG AS YOU TRY TO BE JUST LIKE HIM

BUT I DIDN'T COME HERE TO SERVE AS A PHONY WIZARD!

I CAME TO BECOME A REAL WIZARD THROUGH MY STUDIES AT THE SCHOOL!

HERE IS A R BETTER EACHER OR YOU HERE.

robably.

HIS MAJESTY IS QUITE WORRIED ABOUT THIS SITUATION...

...WITH THE MISSING MASTER WIZARD.

WHAT?

Oh?

I WILL DO MY BEST TO ENSURE THAT YOU ARE ABLE TO TEND TO YOUR COURSES AT THE SAME TIME.

PLEASE! HELP US.

.....

I UNDERSTAND. AND I WILL DO MY BEST.

.....

ALTHOUGH I MADE A PROMISE...

...I OFTEN WONDER— CAN I REALLY DO THIS?

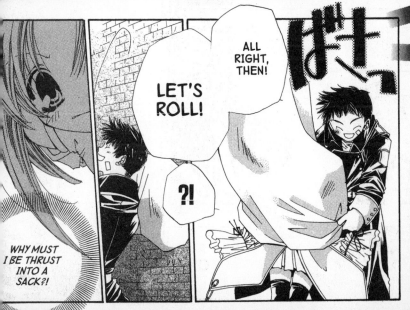

OH! PLEASE WAIT!

STOP MAKING FUN OF ME!

stomp stomp stomp

...THAT MASTER SYLTHFARN HAS RETURNED?!

I HEARD...

NOW WHO IS HE?!

OH.

MINISTER DIPLOMAS?!

WE CAN ALL BREATHE A SIGH OF RELIEF NOW!

Uh-oh. What's this?!

squeeze

I'M SO GLAD YOU'RE BACK SAFE!

AM I DOING OKAY?

SURELY HE SEES RIGHT THROUGH ME!

PLEASE ACCEPT MY APOLOGY.

I DO WISH YOU HADN'T WORRIED.

HE'S SIMPLY EXHAUSTED, YOU KNOW? FOR HE ONLY JUST ARRIVED!

Right?

W-W-WELL...

OH DEAR GOD!

WAIT...

MASTER, WHAT HAPPENED TO YOUR VOICE?

WELL THEN, I'M OFF.

OF COURSE! I UNDERSTAND.

YES! THAT'S RIGHT.

UNTIL THEN, REST AS MUCH AS YOU NEED.

BUT PLEASE DO BE SURE TO FILL ME IN ON YOUR ADVENTURES LATER!

EVEN SO, EVERYTHING IS FINE NOW.

I can't believe he came in here so suddenly!

MY GOD, THAT WAS CLOSE!

WE SIMPLY NEED YOU TO LEARN MORE DETAILS ABOUT SYLTH.

THAT WON'T BE ENOUGH!

I KNOW. I WASN'T PREPARED FOR THAT.

YOUR NAME IS MERLEAW, CORRECT?

MINE IS YUE. AND I'M A FOLLOWER OF THE GREAT MASTER SYLTHFARN.

Y... YES!

THEREFORE, I MUST THANK YOU FOR ACCEPTING THIS TASK.

AND WHILE WE DESPERATELY NEED YOUR HELP...

BUT I DEMAND YOU DO IT WELL!

!

...WHAT GOOD IS IT IF YOU PLAN ON CONTINUING WITH SUCH A HALF-HEARTED ATTITUDE?

I UNDER-
STAND COM-
PLETELY.

YUE!

SHE IS
DOING US
A GREAT
SERVICE.
THERE IS
NO NEED
TO BE SO
HARD ON
HER.

*ALL IS
MEANINGLESS
UNLESS I DO
A FLAWLESS
JOB.*

NO, NO.
HE IS
RIGHT.

*HE SPEAKS
ONLY THE
TRUTH.*

HE TRULY IS.

ALL
RIGHT.
THEN...

FOR YOU
MUST BE
READY TO
ATTEND
THE DINNER
PARTY NEXT
WEEK.

...LET US
CONSTRUCT
A SERIES OF
LESSONS TO
MAKE YOU
THE PERFECT
IMPOSTER.

The Story:

An accident at a museum endows 11-year-old Ichigo Momomiya with the DNA of wildcats. Her new powers are put to the test when she is asked to join a secret group and given the task of protecting the Earth from an unseen enemy.

The Creator:

Mia Ikumi & Reiko Yoshida

ACTION   SCI-FI

Y
YOUTH
AGE 10+

MRP:

$5.99

EARTH

EARTH...
A BEAUTIFUL,
BLUE PLANET
FILLED WITH
MILLIONS
OF LIFE FORMS.

TODAY,
HOWEVER,
THERE ARE
AROUND
2,580 SPECIES
OF ANIMALS
FACING EXTINCTION
ON THIS PLANET.

IT IS TIME
TO STAND UP
AGAINST
THIS
DESTRUCTION...

...NOW.

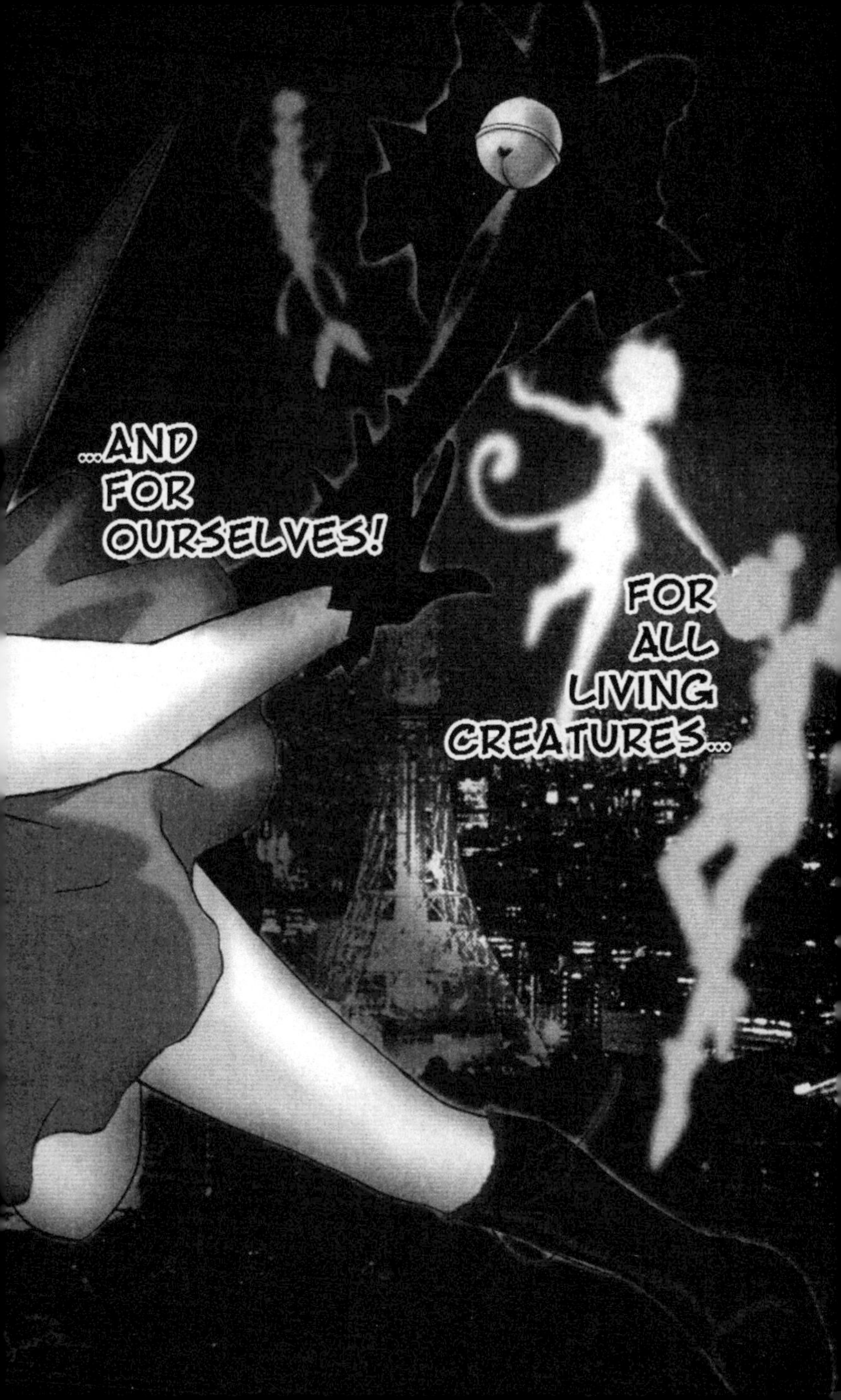

FOR ALL LIVING CREATURES...
...AND FOR OURSELVES!

I DIDN'T EXPECT YOU TO...

OH, UM, I THINK IT'S SO IMPORTANT TO SAVE THE PLANET!

HUH?

I WANTED TO KNOW MORE ABOUT YOU...

...INVITE ME TO THE ENDANGERED SPECIES EXHIBIT.

I AGREE.

Yes!

He's so cute!

AND POPULAR AT SCHOOL BUT...

HE'S VERY ATHLETIC.

Every things gonna be all~

basketball player

HE'S SMART, HE'S CUTE...

WHAT I LIKE BEST IS HIS SMILE!!

Twinkle, Twinkle

Even if this is just a boring exhibit in a gloomy museum...

I don't care where I am... as long as we're together.

LET'S GO CHECK OUT THE WOLVES.

SURE!

47

48

HUH...?

WHAAAT?!

UH...

...GOSH!

49

I WASN'T EXPECTING TO KISS HIM...

I ALWAYS WANTED TO HOLD HANDS WITH HIM, BUT...

I'M SO SORRY... DO YOU HAVE SOME TISSUES?

ICHIGO!

Maybe he likes me!

What is it?

MASAYA...

I JUST THOUGHT ...

GIGGLE

WASTING TISSUE PAPER LEADS TO DEFORESTATION.

YES?

50

PLEASE, USE THIS.

THANK YOU...

WE'RE OKAY.

OH, NO!

THIS HANKIE IS MADE FROM RECYCLED FIBERS!

WHAT NOW?!?

MASAYA,

SEE THIS?

What was her sneer about?

BEAUTIFUL!

51

And how do I get my feelings across to him?

HOW CAN HE POSSIBLY BE SO DENSE?

HE CAN BE SO DUMB!

I'LL BE RIGHT HERE!

I'M GOING TO GET SOMETHING TO DRINK.

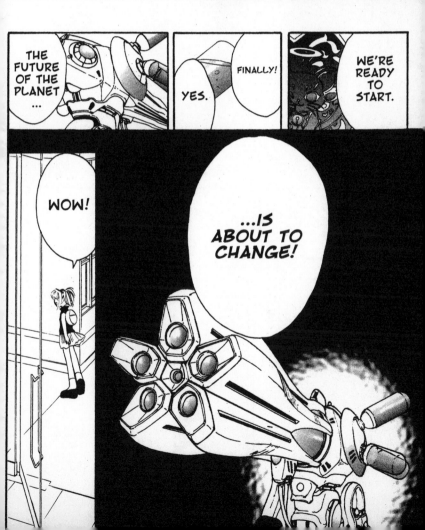

THE FUTURE OF THE PLANET...

YES.

FINALLY!

WE'RE READY TO START.

WOW!

...IS ABOUT TO CHANGE!

MARK OF THE SUCCUBUS

BY ASHLY RAITI & IRENE FLORES

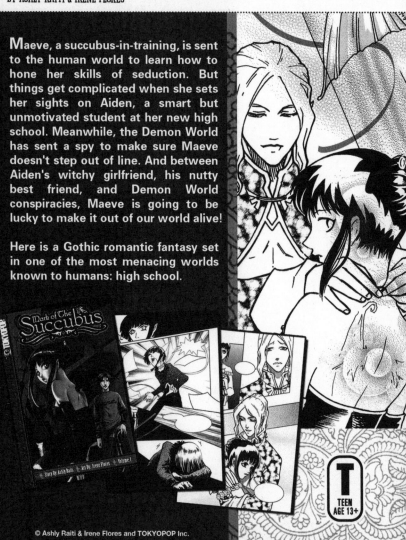

Maeve, a succubus-in-training, is sent to the human world to learn how to hone her skills of seduction. But things get complicated when she sets her sights on Aiden, a smart but unmotivated student at her new high school. Meanwhile, the Demon World has sent a spy to make sure Maeve doesn't step out of line. And between Aiden's witchy girlfriend, his nutty best friend, and Demon World conspiracies, Maeve is going to be lucky to make it out of our world alive!

Here is a Gothic romantic fantasy set in one of the most menacing worlds known to humans: high school.

Mark of The Succubus

Story By: Ashly Raiti · Art By: Irene Flores · Volume 1

© Ashly Raiti & Irene Flores and TOKYOPOP Inc.

T TEEN AGE 13+

FOR MORE INFORMATION VISIT: WWW.TOKYOPOP.CO.UK

The Story:

Guilt-Na-Zan is a vampire aristocrat who was sealed into a cross by Kyoji's ancestor more than 100 years ago. Now Kyoji has revived him—although he was resurrected as a doll and can only transform into his real figure when he sucks blood from Kyoji's sister Tonae... But when you combine Goth clothes and hot vampires, slowly but surely everyone will start to feel like one big family!

The Creator:

Erika Kari

COMEDY   HORROR

T

TEEN
AGE 13+

RP:

9.99

"THERE WAS ONCE A VAMPIRE ARISTOCRAT WHO RULED THE NIGHT IN EUROPE."

"AMONGST HIS DARK POWERS WERE THE ABILITIES TO CONTROL THE BEASTS OF THE EARTH AND CALL THUNDER FROM THE SKY."

SO SAYS THE RECORD OF THE EXORCIST KYOEISAI YOTOBARI.

"AT LAST, WE WERE ABLE TO SEAL HIS SOUL IN A CROSS."

"FOR YEARS, WE STRUGGLED TO DESTROY HIM BY BORROWING GOD'S POWER."

21ST CENTURY, JAPAN

64

YONEN BUZZ

The Story:

Four young musicians—Jun, Sayuri, Keigo, and Atsushi—stand at a new threshold of their career. With the band they created in high school set on a path to rock 'n roll stardom, will the demands of jobs, schoolwork, and relationships get in the way? This musical drama is set for an unforgettable rock odyssey.

The Creator:

Christina Plaka

DRAMA

T

TEEN
AGE 13+

SRP:
$6.99

YEAH, BUT THAT WAS A LONG TIME AGO. WHY ARE YOU ASKING?

IS IT TRUE THAT YOU KISSED THE GIRLS FROM RAN?

IMAI, IS IT TRUE WHAT MIYAKE-SAN SAID?

...YUKA!

AH, NO BIG DEAL. JUST WONDER-ING...

THE WAY HE TALKS, THE WAY HE MOVES... AND HE HAS SUCH BEAUTIFUL HANDS.

I LOVE HIS HAIR AND HIS DARK EYES...

...HIS COOL STYLE AND HIS LEAN BOD.

WHY SHOULD I BE SURPRISED? A HOT, TALENTED GUY LIKE HIM...

...WOULD NEVER BE INTERESTED IN A PLAIN, AVERAGE GIRL LIKE ME.

HE SEEMS SO UNATTAINABLE, EVEN THOUGH WE WORK SO CLOSE EVERY DAY.

I WONDER WHAT HE THINKS ABOUT ME.

I'M SURE HE JUST SEES ME AS THE NICE LITTLE GIRL NEXT DOOR.

WELL, HE JUST TURNED 20 AND I'M GOING TO BE 14...

 I'M SURE HE'S ATTRACTED TO OLDER WOMEN...

WHY IS THIS SO HARD?

IF ONLY I KNEW HOW TO MAKE HIM NOTICE ME...

SEE YOU LATER!

I REALLY MISSED THIS...

IT FEELS GREAT TO HAVE A COUPLE OF HOURS OFF.

TAP

BYE HISAO-KUN.

BSCH
DOK
DSCH
DOK
BSCH
DSCH
BSCH

THAT'S SOME WICKED DRUMMING!

WH-WHERE IS THAT COMING FROM?